Creative Cloth Doll Making

Creative Cloth Doll Making

New Approaches for Using Fibers, Beads, Dyes, and Other Exciting Techniques

GLOUCESTER MASSACHUSETTS

ROCKPORT
PUBLISHERS

Patti Medaris Culea

Designed by Peter King & Company

First published in the United States of America by:
Rockport Publishers, Inc.
33 Commercial Street
Gloucester, MA 01930-5089

ISBN 1-56496-942-8
10 9

Design and Layout: Peter King & Company
Cover Design: Peter King & Company
Cover Image: Bobbie Bush Photography,
www.bobbiebush.com
Doll Portraits: Bobbie Bush Photography,
www.bobbiebush.com
Step Photography: Hirsch Design
Step Illustrator: Judy Love
Pattern Illustrator: Roberta Frauwirth
Project Manager/Copy Editor: Stacey Ann Follin
Proofreader: Karen Comerford

Library of Congress Cataloging-in-Publication Data
Medaris Culea, Patti.
  Creative cloth doll making : new approaches for using fibers, beads, dyes, and other exciting techniques / Patti Medaris Culea.
    p. cm.
  ISBN 1-56496-942-8 (pbk.)
  1. Dollmaking. 2. Cloth dolls. I. Title.
TT175 .M46 2003
745.592'21—dc21   2002014943

Printed in Singapore

Contents

Introduction

*"High is our calling, friend!
Creative art demands the service
of a mind and heart, though
sensitive, yet, in their weakest
part, heroically fashioned."*

William Wordsworth

Creative doll making. These words are at the center of what defines us as doll makers. We are artists who have a passion to create. If others like·or appreciate what we do, fine. If not, the love of what we do sustains us. As artists, we think outside the box, whereas others keep within what is familiar. There is no way to predict when our inspirations will come or where they will come from, but when they arrive, we frantically search for the nearest scratch pad.

This book is for people who know they have the gift of artistic creativity and want to take their doll-making talents to a higher level. It's also for those who have recently discovered a yearning to be creative—for those who never thought they could be doll makers. It's my hope that this book enables you to start with a published pattern and make a doll that's unique. I want to help you learn to create a doll that has your signature, a doll that is truly yours.

Being creative goes beyond scratch pads, needles, thread, sewing machines, and colored pencils. It begins when we rise in the morning. The creative person reflects their calling in the way they dress, cook, go to work, look at the world, interact with others, and think.

This is more than a book about doll making. I hope it will help you integrate creative techniques into many areas of your life—and allow you to take new risks, let go, and have fun! For example, rubber stamps and paints aren't new, but using them on already-made cloth figures is a fresh concept. Tyvek has been around for years, mainly for envelopes and environmental suits, but here you'll see how it can be used to create whimsical clothing and beads. And beading! What a wonderful art form. You'll see that when beads are used to embellish a cloth doll, your creation can become magical. Free-motion machine embroidery has been used to create wonderful garments for adults; you'll discover how to use it to change the look of fabric for doll clothing, shoes, wings, and bodices. Fabric collage is commonly found in quilting and garments, but it's also an exciting technique for making doll bodies and clothing.

This book contains patterns for three doll bodies and also for accessories. The doll pattern pieces are designed so that you can mix and match body parts as you wish. In each chapter, after the main doll project is introduced and described in detail, there is a gallery section where family, friends, and colleagues have interpreted the same patterns in their own style. You'll see the work of beginning doll makers, intermediate doll makers, and some "Hall of Fame" artists, too! This will give you lots of inspiration for making a doll that's uniquely yours.

This book is for you, the reader. I hope you enjoy reading each page as an adventure in creativity. Our world is one of heads, threads, beads, and the seeds of new ideas. I'm sure many of you will use the book to come up with new and exciting techniques. I hope you will share your creations with me and with others in the wonderful world of doll making. More than anything, I hope that you'll have fun.

Patti Culea

The Basics

Exploring key techniques

1

Art projects begin with basic techniques. Doll making is no different. An understanding and appreciation of those techniques will help in your creative process and enable you to take full advantage of the methods presented in each chapter.

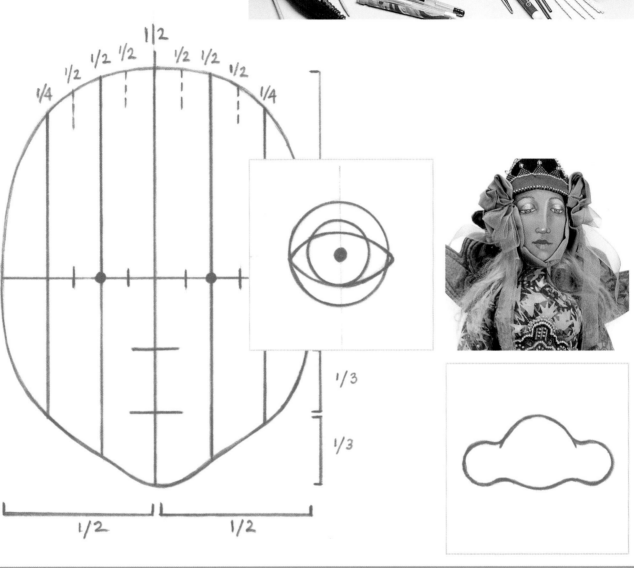

Gathering the Necessary Supplies

Doll making has changed dramatically over the past several years, with new techniques, supplies, and materials being discovered every day. Many supplies that doll makers use come from places like hardware stores and thrift shops; others come simply from the imaginations of the doll makers themselves.

Just as carpenters and plumbers have toolboxes to house and transport their essential tools, doll makers must have a basic sewing kit. You'll need it at home and, when you travel, to take to classes.

The Basic Kit

Work Space Essentials

Container for water

Containers for mixing dyes and paints

Cover-up or old clothes to wear

Fabric eraser

Hemostats—for turning and stuffing

Large and small finger-turning tools

Latex or plastic gloves

Measuring tape

Mechanical pencil

Paper towels

Plastic work surface

Sewing machine (your closest friend); cleaned and oiled and with a new needle

Sponges—small and large

Stuffing forks

Sweater rack for your clothes dryer or a hair dryer for setting paints and dyes

Cutting Tools

Paper and/or craft scissors

Pinking shears

Rotary cutter with extra blades

Rotary mat

Sharp scissors for cutting curves

Small scissors for cutting out fingers

Needles and Pins

Embroidery needles, tapestry needles (have one with the end of the eye cut off for making ribbon roses), a 3" (7.5 cm) doll-sculpting needle

Hand-sewing needles; long darning needles and/or quilter's basting needles

Machine needles—sharps in sizes 10, 12, metallic, embroidery, and topstitch

Needle threader with a cutter

Pincushion with straight pins

Safety pins

Threads

Decorative threads, such as metallic, rayon, and polyester threads

Good-quality polyester threads for your machine and hand sewing

Strong quilter's thread and/or upholstery thread for sculpting

Art Supplies

Colored pencils—preferably Prismacolor pencils (These work better on fabric than other brands.)

Gel Pens—white, black, red, colors of choice for eyes

Sulky's Ultra Solvy (a water-soluble stabilizer) or Craft Mistress Romeo (for those in the United Kingdom or "down under")

Zig Millennium pens in nib size 0.005, in brown, black, red; Micron Pigma Pens (Most other pens bleed on fabric.)

Body Supplies

High-quality cream- or white-colored pima cotton

Fairfield's Polyfil Stuffing

Pipe cleaners for wiring fingers

Hair Supplies

Felting needles

Mohair

Strips of fabric

Yarn

Dyeing and Painting Supplies

Colorhue Silk Dyes by Things Japanese

"Impress Me" rubber stamps by Sherrill Kahn

Jacquard's Dye-NA-Flow paints

Jacquard's Lumiere paints

Jacquard's Pearl-EX pigments

Jacquard's Textile paints

Margarita salt (available at grocery stores)

Rock salt

Wide round and flat brushes in sizes 10, 12, and 14

Special Effects Supplies

Beads—size 11 seed beads, accent beads

Fancy yarns for creating freeform clothing and embellishments

Silk caps—available at weaving stores

Laying Out Patterns

Before sewing any patterns in this book, look over the pattern pieces. Some have tracing and sewing lines, others have seam allowances. For the pieces that have tracing and sewing lines, trace onto the wrong side of the fabric, double the fabric, and sew. For the other patterns, either trace onto the wrong side of the fabric, double the fabric, and cut out, or make templates, trace, and cut out. Just remember to look at the pattern pieces before jumping in and sewing.

The head patterns have an arrow, which should be lined up with the grain of the fabric. The grain runs along the selvage of the fabric. The selvage is in line with the finished end of the fabric, not the cut end. This is important because it puts the stretch of the fabric where the cheeks are, so when you fill the doll's head with stuffing, it will have a nice plump face, rather than a long, skinny one.

1. Lay out the paper pattern on a table—a light table if you have one. Lay your fabric on top of the paper pattern, with the wrong side of fabric facing you. Using a mechanical pencil, trace all pattern pieces. Trace the darts, too. Double the fabric, and pin it in several places. For pattern pieces that don't have tracing and sewing lines, simply cut the pieces out. For those that have the lines, sew the pieces, and then cut them out.

2. For larger body parts and the legs, use pinking shears to cut them out to avoid the need to go around clipping curves. Avoid using pinking shears for the face and hands because these parts are too small.

AUTHOR'S SUGGESTION

I use a Bernina sewing machine. My normal stitch length is 2.0. When sewing the hands and face on a doll, I lower my stitch length to 1.5. That way I have clean seams and I can sew two stitches between fingers and across the tips of each finger. This also ensures a strong seam that won't burst open. When cutting out the hands, after they are sewn, I leave a scant ⅛" (0.3 cm) seam allowance. For the rest of the body, I leave a full ⅛" (0.3 cm) seam allowance.

3. When sewing the hands and face, use a shorter stitch length on your machine.

4. When sewing the doll's body parts, note the openings. These are important when putting the parts together and turning them right side out. Some pattern pieces have tabs that provide extra fabric for folding down so that it's easier to create a clean hand-sewn seam.

5. After sewing the body parts together, you'll turn the body parts right side out. (Note that the steps for doing this vary depending on the particular project.) Hemostats work well for this step, for everything but fingers. Reach in with the hemostats, grab the end of the foot, leg, or other body part and pull. Use the closed end of the hemostats to go back in and smooth out curves.

Turning Fingers

Although turning fingers does take practice, certain tools are available to make the process easier. You can buy an Itsy Bitsy Finger Turning kit created for doing just that (see Resources, page 118), or you can improvise and buy a couple of tubes from a hobby store that carries model train supplies. The tubes come in various widths; $1/16$", $3/32$", $5/32$", and $1/8$" (0.2 to 0.3 cm) are good for turning fingers. Just keep in mind that the tubes come in 12" (30.5 cm) lengths, so you'll need to cut them in half first.

If you're using the tubes, begin by inserting the largest tube inside a finger. Then, using the smallest tube, turn over the seam allowance, and push against the finger. Pull the finger up onto the smaller tube. The pressure against the seam allowance will help push the finger inside the hand.

You'll need two hands to do this, so hold the larger tube against your stomach. After you turn each finger, reach in with your hemostats, and turn the hand and then arm right side out.

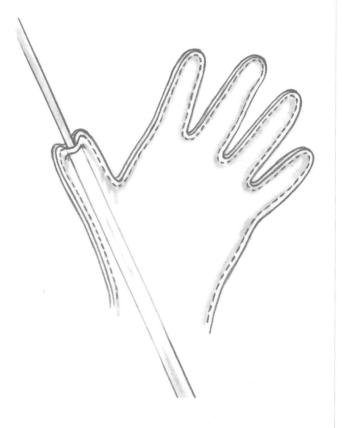

Begin by inserting
the largest tube inside a finger.

AUTHOR'S SUGGESTION

If this is your first time turning fingers this way, be patient. Although this step takes practice, it's worth learning because it helps prevent the seams at the fingers from bursting open. If they do, don't worry: That finger will determine which is your left or right hand because you'll use that side for the fingernail. More on that later.

Stuffing Body Parts

Use whichever stuffing you prefer, but avoid the type that feels like cotton because this type doesn't sculpt well. When stuffing body parts, except the hands, grab as much stuffing as you can to fit through the opening, and feed the stuffing into the part. Larger bunches of stuffing give a smooth look; smaller bunches, a lumpy look.

To stuff a body part, start by pushing the stuffing into the outside of the part first, and then fill up the inside. This technique helps prevent wrinkling. For small parts like the nose, place a small amount there, and then continue filling in with large amounts of stuffing.

When stuffing the hands, use a stuffing fork to place small amounts of stuffing in the fingers and then hemostats to fill up the hand and arm. (See Resources, page 118, for more information on stuffing forks.)

For a more realistic look, you can insert pipe cleaners into the fingers to give the appearance that the doll has bones in her hands. Pinch back both ends of all pipe cleaners. Bend four pipe cleaners in half, placing one end in one finger and the other end in the finger next to it, until every finger has a pipe cleaner. The pipe cleaners should be in line with each other. The two straight pipe cleaners are for the thumbs. Place these in the thumbs.

To complete the look, push the arm fabric down, and wrap the thumb pipe cleaner around the two bent ends of the pipe cleaners in the doll's fingers, allowing some of the pipe cleaner to stick up in the arm. If the fingers look like they need just a bit more stuffing, you can insert it now. Push back the fabric, and wrap the stuffing around the stuffing fork so it looks like a cotton swab, and then insert it into a finger. Next fill the palm side of each hand with stuffing, and continue filling up the arms around the pipe cleaner.

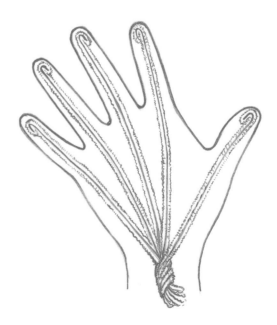

Wrap the thumb pipe cleaner around the two bent ends of the pipe cleaners in the doll's fingers.

Creating the Face

Most people find creating the face to be the most challenging—or even intimidating—task when it comes to doll making, but once you learn how to place features and find out which materials work best, you won't fear faces again. After all, you don't need to be an artist to create the face you want on a doll: You simply need to relax, have some fun, and let your creativity flow.

Human faces are designed perfectly for drawing because they're grafted out. For a doll's face, all that's needed are a few lines to create the foundation for the details.

1. To graft the face, start by drawing a line lengthwise down the center of the face with a mechanical pencil. (Note that you don't need to do this on the faces that have a seam down the center.)

2. Next, draw a line at the halfway point between the forehead and the chin.

3. Slice off about one-quarter at each side of the face.

4. Half each side of the face again. This creates the center for the eyes and outside corners of the mouth.

5. Halve each half again. This designates where the inside and outside corners of the eyes will be.

6. Below the half mark widthwise, split the rest of the face in thirds. This provides the basic graft for placing features. The rest of the features are made up of circles and ovals. For a male doll, use more squares than circles. The eyes are drawn first because most features are created from points on the eyes.

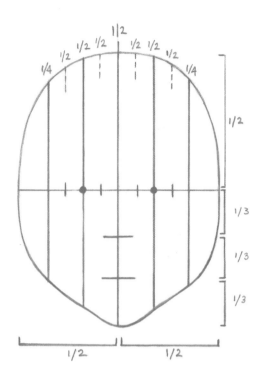

[step 6]
Below the half mark widthwise,
split the rest of the face in thirds.

AUTHOR'S SUGGESTION

If you're right-handed, draw the left side first; if you're left-handed, do the opposite. By drawing the weak side first, it's much easier to match the strong side. First, square off where you'll place the eyes, then just below the halfway line widthwise, place a line.

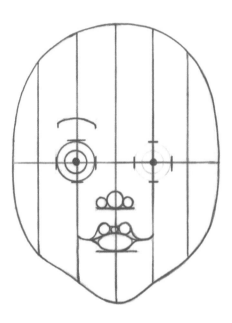

Now you can draw the eyes,
which are simply three circles.

Next draw the upper eyelid.

The Eyes

Next measure the distance between the center line and each line on either side of that center line. This measurement determines the height and width of the eye. Faces should be 5 eye-widths wide, with 1 eye-width in between each eye. Grafting out the face helps guarantee the accuracy of this measurement. Now you can draw the eyes, which are simply three circles. The large circle, which fits inside the "box" that you created, becomes the eyeball. Inside that first circle is another circle, which represents the iris, or the colored part of the eye. Inside the second circle is the third and smallest circle, which represents the pupil.

Next draw the upper eyelid. Start at the inside corner of the eye at the halfway line. Curve the eyelid to touch the iris, and then continue the curve to the outside of the eyeball at the halfway mark. Depending on the look you're after, the lower lid can touch the iris or leave a bit of the eyeball showing.

The eyebrows are $1/4$" to $1/3$" (0.6 to 0.8 cm) above the eyes. They start straight up from the inside corner of the eye and extend to the outside corner. To achieve the full brow, draw a slightly curved line to connect these points.

The Nose

The nose is also made up of three circles. One large circle is drawn on the center line and above, but touching, the one-third line you drew when you split the face. On either side of the nose, keeping inside the one-quarter line, draw two smaller circles. Draw in the nostrils.

The Mouth

The mouth is made up of three circles, an oval, and wavy lines. First, draw two dots straight down from the pupils on the one-third line for the mouth. Draw a small circle at the center of the mouth. On either side of this circle draw larger circles, again keeping within the one-quarter line. Underneath these three circles draw an oval.

Draw a wavy line at the center of the mouth, starting at the milk bud and curving up and around the larger circles on either side. To finish the upper lip, start at the center and curve up and around the circles and down to the outside corners of the mouth. Follow the same sequence for the lower lip, referring to the illustration on the right as needed.

Stand back and look at the face, then make any necessary adjustments. Just keep in mind that slight variations are what make a doll's face unique, so don't get too focused on perfectly lining up the eyes when human eyes aren't perfectly aligned themselves. Because pencil marks will disappear when you color the face, you'll need to create a permanent outline. So once you're satisfied with the placement of the eyelids, irises, pupils, nostrils, and lips, outline them with a brown pen (for example, a Micron Pigma or Zig Millennium pen). After you've outlined everything, erase all pencil marks.

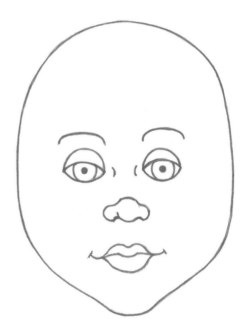

Each subsequent chapter includes additional details for coloring and sculpting the various doll faces. Although each face is different, the basic principles are referred to as each doll is explained. Also, notice how each doll maker in the Gallery sections interprets the basic patterns and techniques in each chapter. You'll see that the variation possibilities are endless!

Surfaces and Coloration

Working with dyes, paints, and stamps

One of the most exciting things you can do is create a beautiful painting from a blank canvas. In doll making, you essentially do the same thing— you transform a blank doll into a beautiful work of art.

This chapter takes you through the steps of making a beginning doll. After you sew her together, she becomes a blank canvas. You'll then embellish this canvas using dyes, paints, and stamps. You'll also learn more details about creating a face for your doll.

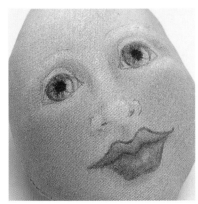

Beginning Doll

The doll featured in this chapter, Willamae (Doll #1), is a perfect project to start with if you're new to doll making. She's constructed from the pattern found on pages 106 and 107. The pattern is simple. Her head is flat, a perfect canvas for learning the basic principles for drawing a face. Her body is formed with only one pattern piece, and her hands and feet are simple silhouettes for easy sewing.

The first layer of design on this doll is a dyed surface. You'll learn to color the body, mixing several dyes to achieve a pretty flesh color, and then to embellish this layer with stamped designs. Feel free to adapt the palette to your liking as a way to start personalizing your design.

Her clothing is made from silk crepe de chine, which is also dyed and stamped. The simple torn pieces are draped into a lovely outfit and embellished with silk ribbons and ribbon roses. It's easy to transform simple scraps of fabric into fabulous garments by wrapping, gathering, and draping the pieces in interesting ways. If you feel ambitious, you can even add shoes to the ensemble, or go without. It's up to you.

Finally, you'll learn, step-by-step, how to continue to add detail to your doll's face, using pencils, gel pens, and rubber stamps.

Supplies

$^1/_4$ *yard (23 cm) pima cotton*

pins

thread to match

scissors

mechanical pencil and soft eraser

stuffing

stuffing tools

hemostats

hand-sewing needles

strong thread for attaching the head, arms, and legs

3" (7.5 cm) needle to attach legs

fabric marking pens: brown, red, black

plastic bag to cover workspace

paper towel

ice cube tray

Jacquard's Dye-NA-Flow paints: white, ecru, ochre, magenta, sun yellow, turquoise

Jacquard's Lumiere paints: super sparkle, silver, turquoise

paper plate and sponge

rubber stamps

$^1/_4$ *yard (23 cm) silk crepe de chine*

eye droppers

3 yards (2.7 m) 7-mm white silk ribbon

matches and a candle

pie plate with water (optional)

beads

colored pencils: sienna brown, cream, white, carmine red, periwinkle, peacock blue, copenhagen blue, scarlet lake

gel pens: black, purple, white

glitzy yarns

[step 4]
Cut a slit on one side of the
head toward the chin.

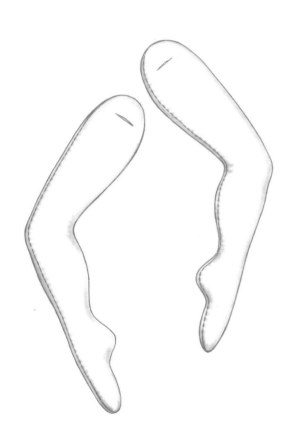

[step 5]
Cut slits toward the top of each leg.

Making the Body

1. Arrange and trace the patterns for Doll #1 onto the wrong side of the body fabric. (See Chapter 1, page 14.) Then double the fabric, right sides together, and pin in several places.

2. Begin sewing the body parts together, leaving a section open, for turning, as indicated on the patterns. *Note:* The head and legs don't have openings; you'll cut a slit later for turning. When sewing the neck, backstitch at the beginning, and then double stitch just the neck sides. This will prevent the seams from busting out.

3. Cut out all body pieces.

4. Cut a slit on one side of the head toward the chin. Make this slit on the side of the head with pencil marks.

5. Cut slits toward the top of each leg. Make sure you have a right leg and a left leg by placing the legs together and positioning the slits on adjacent sides.

6. Turn all pieces, right sides out.

7. This step is optional, but it gives the finished doll a nice look: Follow the markings on the hand template to trace in fingers on the hands and topstitch by machine. Do this before filling up the doll body with stuffing. When topstitching, do a backstitch at the beginning and end of each finger, to keep any threads from coming loose while stuffing.

8. Use the stuffing to fill the main body first. Fill the doll until it feels firm, especially the neck. Fill the head next. Smooth out any wrinkles in the fabric by filling with more stuffing.

9. Place the head on the neck by grabbing the neck with your hemostats and pushing it up into the opening at the back of the head. Pin in place. Thread a regular hand-sewing needle with ¼-yard (46 cm) of strong thread. Place a knot in the end. Ladder stitch the head to the neck. Anchor the thread at the back of the head, and cut.

10. Stuff the legs. After the legs are filled, ladder stitch the openings closed with a needle and thread.

11. Thread a 3" (7.5 cm) needle with 2 yards (1.8 m) of strong thread. Put a knot in the end of the thread, and attach to the side of the hip.

12. Place the leg at the hip, and attach by running a threaded needle through the leg. Go back through the leg, over to the other side, and through the other leg. Go back and forth at least three times, then anchor the thread at the inside of the hip (under a leg).

13. Fill the arms with stuffing, starting with the fingers, using the stuffing fork. Finish filling the arms with stuffing to ¼" (0.6 cm) below the opening. Sew a gathering stitch along the top of each arm. Push the raw edges of the fabric inside as you do this. Tack the arm to the side of the body at the shoulders with a stitch.

14. Repeat for the other arm. The doll is now ready to be dyed, stamped, and clothed.

[step 7]
Follow the markings on the hand template to trace in fingers on the hands and topstitch by machine.

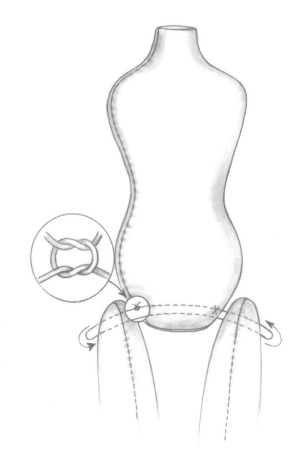

[step 11]
Put a knot in the end of the thread, and attach to the side of the hip.

Drawing the Face

Before dyeing, draw in the facial features. (See "Drawing Faces," pages 17 to 19.) Outline all drawn features with a brown fabric marking pen.

Adding Color with Dye

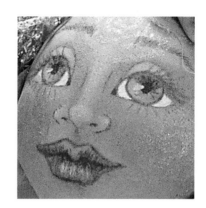

Jacquard's Dye-NA-Flow paints dye just about any fiber but polyester. When used straight from the container, they keep their color; however, when diluted, they do fade a bit. They don't change the "hand," or feel, of the fabric. They're also nontoxic; therefore, they don't have harmful fumes or much of an odor, so it's unnecessary to wear goggles or a mask when using them.

These paints should be heat set—and, fortunately, that's quite simple to do. If you have a sweater rack for your clothes dryer, set the dryer for cotton, place the dyed doll body on the rack, and dry for 30 minutes. If you don't have a sweater rack, use your hair dryer or a heat gun (found at stamp stores and hardware stores). You can also use an iron to set the colors. When dyeing a doll that isn't going to be laundered, heat setting is unnecessary. Heat setting simply guarantees that the colors won't fade.

To set up a dye space, gather an ice cube tray, some brushes, a container for water, paper towels, and a plastic garbage bag.

1. Lay down the plastic bag to cover the workspace. Next put a layer of paper towels on top of the plastic. The towels will catch any spills and are good for dabbing the brush on when doing some of the dry-brush techniques.

2. Pour a teaspoon of each dye into the different sections of the ice cube tray. Leave a few sections empty for mixing colors together.

3. To create a flesh color, add 1 teaspoon of white, then add a drop at a time of ecru and ochre until you get the shade of flesh you want. Add a drop of magenta to this mixture and a little sun yellow. If the color is too dark, add a bit of water and more white.

4. Brush this mixture onto the flesh parts of the doll body. Working quickly, add other colors, as desired, to cover the entire body. Work quickly because the dyes dry fast, and if you go back and paint next to a dry spot, it will produce a watermark.

5. For cheek color, place a small amount of a skin-toned dye in an empty space of the ice cube tray, and add some magenta. Pick up a small amount of dye on your brush, and dab onto a paper towel to remove excess. Brush her cheeks with this color. The color should bleed.

26

Making Clothes

Use silk or cotton for clothing. In the featured doll, silk crepe de chine is used.

1. Wet a piece of the silk crepe de chine thoroughly with plain tap water. Squeeze out excess water.

2. Place small amounts of sun yellow, turquoise, and magenta into the ice cube tray that you used earlier. Scrunch up the silk, and dip into the yellow. With eye droppers, drop magenta and turquoise onto the remaining white areas of the silk. Squeeze out excess dye, and hang the fabric up to dry. Let the colors set for 24 hours, then iron the silk with a warm iron.

3. Using the eye dropper technique only, color the silk ribbons. Ribbons are much narrower than the fabric, so the piece could get too saturated by dipping it into one color first.

Adding Interest with Stamps

When working with stamps, dab on just a bit of the paint with a sponge. Pick up some paint on the sponge, then dab off any extra paint onto your pallet, thus enabling you to put just the right amount of paint onto the stamp. Have water and an old toothbrush handy; the paints dry quickly and can ruin the stamps if not cleaned as soon as you finish stamping.

Experiment with several colors of paint on a stamp. The colors will bleed together to create other colors. For instance, yellow and blue will make green where the two colors meet, creating some interesting effects.

1. Using the Lumiere paints, place a dollop of each color onto a paper plate. Pick up some paint on a sponge, and dab onto a stamp. Immediately stamp the doll's body. Continue this stamping process until you have the effect you want.

2. Let the paints dry thoroughly. Set an iron to the cotton setting. Set the paints by lightly ironing over the body parts.

4. Once the fabric is dry, measure the doll's body, and decide how long you want her skirt to be. Tear the fabric to the desired length. (The featured doll's skirt measures 18" x 4" [45.5 x 10 cm]). Light a candle, and carefully run the torn edge along the flame to seal the edge.

5. Using the Lumiere paints and stamps, create designs on the silk. The silk can be stamped before or after it's dyed.

6. For the bodice, tear two strips of fabric 10" x 1½" (25.5 x 4 cm). Wrap these two around each other as shown below.

[step 6]
Wrap these two strips
around each other.

7. Bring one side up over her shoulders and the other side around to her back. With a needle and thread, tack in place at the back. On one shoulder, tear a long strip of silk, 10" x ½" (25.5 x 1.3 cm), and tie it in various places. Then loop the strip, and tack it to her shoulder. Create some silk ribbon roses or other flowers, and sew these to her bodice. (See the photo on page 23 for ideas.)

8. Her skirt is one long strip of fabric, 18" x 4" (45.5 x 10 cm). With right sides together, sew up the back seam, along the 4" (10 cm) edges. Then gather the waist by hand with a running stitch. Slip the skirt onto her body, and pull the threads to fit the waist. Tack in place.

9. The upper skirt is another strip of fabric, 18" x 4" (45.5 x 10 cm), folded over to create a double ruffle. Hand-gather at the center, and pull the threads to fit at the waist. Leave open at the center.

10. Stamp on her body and her clothing. Add some silk ribbons at her waist and a silk ribbon rose.

Adding Shoes

1. Trace four shoe patterns onto the wrong side of the silk scrap (left over from the skirt and top). Two are for the outside of the shoes, and two are for the lining. Double the fabric, and sew along the solid line, leaving open where marked.

2. Cut out all pieces, and turn two of them right side out. Place the two lining pieces inside the other two, and pin in place with right sides together. Sew along the raw edges from the back of the shoe all the way around. To turn the shoes right side out, cut a slit in the lining at the bottom in the seam, then turn right side out. Finger-press along edges, and slip the shoes onto her feet.

3. Fold a 12" (30.5 cm) length of silk ribbon in half, and tack at the center of the top of the shoe. Bring the ribbon to the back of the shoe, and tack in place. Wrap the ribbons around her ankles as shown in the photo on page 23, then tie in front, just above her ankle, in a bow. Tack in place. Hide the knot under the shoe top. Add some beads at the center top of shoe where the silk ribbon is attached.

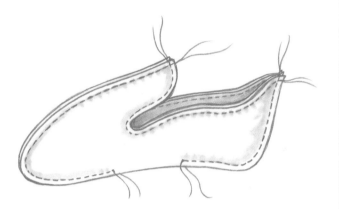

[step 1]
Double the fabric, and sew along the solid line, leaving open where marked.

AUTHOR'S SUGGESTION

The shoes are an optional embellishment. Some of the artists who made dolls from this pattern chose not to make shoes; others did.

Finishing the Face

1. Assemble colored pencils, gel pens, and fabric pens.

2. Start by shading the various parts of the face. Using the sienna brown pencil, start by shading the temple, above the eye crease, down the sides of the nose, under her nose, in the upper lip, down one side of the lower lip, and under the lower lip.

3. With the cream pencil, color in next to the brown. The face will start to curve upward and catch light. The cream creates this effect on a flat-faced doll. Use the cream to color just a bit under each eye and along her upper lip.

4. Using the white pencil, lighten the forehead, the center of the nose, across the ball of the nose and each flare, and the center of the chin. Before blending, brighten up her cheeks with the carmine red pencil.

5. Blend all of this pencil work with a scrap of fabric.

The Lips

1. The lips use two shades of red. Color in both upper and lower lips with carmine red, then use scarlet lake to darken the upper lip and down one side of the lower lip. Darken a bit of the lower lip along the bottom edge.

2. Lighten the center of her lower lip with the white pencil. Outline both upper and lower lips with the red gel roller or fabric pen. Use a brown fabric pen to outline the center of her lips.

The Eyes

The eyes can be created using three shades of one color or three different colors. For this doll, three different blues are used—periwinkle, peacock blue, and copenhagen blue.

1. Using the lightest shade first, fill in the irises. To evoke light hitting the doll's face from her left, make that side of her eyes lighter. Using the medium shade, color in under her upper eyelid and down the side of the eye that's in the shadow. Using the darkest shade, color in just under the eyelid. With the white pencil, lighten the side of the eye that's catching the light.

2. Blacken the pupils with the black gel roller. Outline the irises with the purple gel roller, and run some spokes out from the pupils.

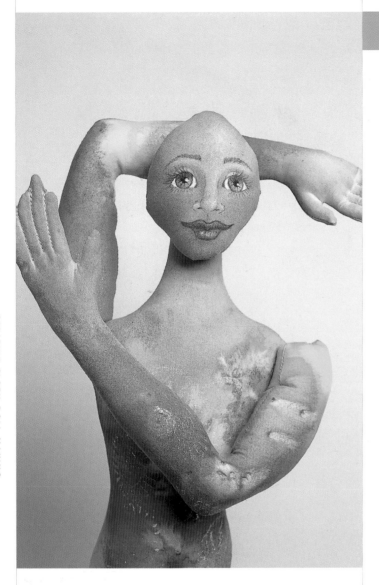

Finishing the Doll

1. Color in the whites of her eyes with the white gel roller. Add a highlight to each pupil on the side that's catching the light. Place a dot of red with a fabric pen or red pencil at the inside corners of each eye to represent the tear duct.

2. Outline her eyelids with the brown fabric pen again. Feather in her eyelashes: Start at the center above the pupil, and draw a short eyelash and then a long one, and alternate between adding a short lash and a long one until you have a pleasing effect. Her lower eyelashes will be shorter and lighter in color. Draw them in with a light touch.

3. The eyebrows are feathered in following the line you drew at the beginning. Always start with the brown pen, and change to black if you feel she needs darker eyebrows and eyelashes.

4. Outline her nostrils and the flare of her nose. Add some more shading and highlights if you feel she needs it. Add eye shadow with other colors.

5. Finish the face with more stamps.

6. For the head piece, loop silk scraps and tack them along her hairline (seam line), and fill in the bald spots with more silk loops. Add a silk ribbon and some glitzy yarns.

Senta's Baggage

ARTIST: Claudia Medaris   (Pattern: Doll #1)

"Senta's Baggage is a rubber-stamped doll. Any rubber stamp is suitable with fabric paints, though larger stamps, or ones with fewer details, tend to make a cleaner image on fabric. I suggest you work with tightly woven fabrics and clean the stamps carefully after each use.

 I coordinated the primary rubber images for this piece with various larger background stamps. Using fabric paint, stamp dabbers, and masking techniques, I embellished the entire surface of the cloth doll with an array of connecting images. I then inked the main foreground stamp with hues of fabric paint. While wet, these paints blend easily when you dab them on the surface of the rubber image."

Pattielise

ARTIST: elinor peace bailey   (Pattern: Doll #1)

"This doll uses a slightly modified version of the Beginner pattern. I used an embellishment technique I learned from Elise Peeples which uses Liquatex Gel Medium, crocheted lace, Gesso and Jacquard paints and dyes. I thought I would call the doll Pattielise. She is organic and seems to grow new horns at every turn in the bend.

It was fun not to have the road mapped out too clearly. Patti, Elise, and I have been making dolls for years, and we were bound to rub off on one another from time to time. This doll shows this with the influence of Patti's dyeing and Elise's collage with a bit of my own drawings and colors thrown in."

Culeoptera

ARTIST: Barbara Chapman   (Pattern: Doll #2)

"I began by painting Culeoptera's body with a generous
coating of Gesso, but then smoke fairies descended
overnight and smeared a layer of charcoal on her
body. [*Author's note*: This charcoal effect was from a
recent house fire that destroyed much of the artist's
beautiful artwork.] Luckily the Gesso layer prevented
most of the smoke from seeping through. I then
painted her with Jacquard's Dye-NA-Flow paints, which,
of course, wouldn't penetrate the fabric in a dyelike fashion because of the Gesso. On parts of her body and
face, I used Lumiere metallic paints.

In dressing her, I wanted to show some of the
body, so I loosely crocheted a sweater for
her and paired it with snazzy handmade
felt pants with velvet cuffs. I created
jazzy metallic stockings by needle
weaving down to the velvet-and-
gold-encrusted shoes. I added lay-
ers of sleeves, collaging surfaces over each other to
create an interesting
effect. I collaged some
sheer lace and calligraphy
papers to her face to create a
contemporary fantasy feel and to
tie in with the textures in the costume.

Culeoptera was a work in progress. Trial
and error with painted leather, needle-
woven stockings, and hair styles took her
through several identity crises, but
everything came together with antique
sari border sequins and gilding. With hair
wound with lace from India, a few collage
elements, and embellishments, she was
done. I named my doll Culeoptera in
honor of Patti Culea, who brought about
her metamorphosis."

Irulan

ARTIST: Janet Beth Cruz (Pattern: Doll #2)

"To start Irulan, I looked through fashion magazines like *Harper's Bazaar* and *Vogue* to find a stylish outfit for my retro doll. Then I focused on the colors. It's always fun to use bright colors, colors that you love but never find yourself wearing or using in your home. For me, it's bright pinks, reds, oranges, and yellows. When I was ready to dye her body, I used Jacquard's Dye-NA-Flow paints—sun yellow, scarlet, bright orange, and hot fuchsia. For her face I used their salmon, ochre, and white. Although you don't see much of her body, it's just as bright as her outfit.

Her shoes were a dilemma. I knew what I wanted but wasn't sure how to achieve it. I finally drew the design on paper. With help from my mom, Patti Medaris Culea, we added seam allowances, and I was ready to make them from fabric. After sewing and stuffing the shoes, I attached them to her feet and embellished them with beads. Irulan carries a hand-dyed purse and lounges on three beanbags. She's ready to pose for any photo shoot."

Leading by a Hare

ARTIST: Margaret (Marge) Clok Gorman (Pattern: Doll #3)

"On the day Patti's pattern arrived, I set my imagination loose to make a doll with no limits for painting, stamping, or dying techniques. I had a hare-brained idea: I wanted the doll to be a rabbit with human characteristics. As I began construction, I chose not to incorporate the moveable joints provided in the pattern and instead ladder stitched the arms and legs for a fully posed doll. I eliminated the bust, and I added ears and a fluffy tail.

My idea was to dye all the body parts except the head and hands. I saturated both sides of the doll from the neck to the feet with a spray bottle filled with water. Next came Jacquard's Dye-NA-Flow paints in green, blue, and purple. I dipped a toothbrush into the purple and spattered it all over the doll. I used the spray bottle again and got an exciting watercolor effect. I repeated the process with red, yellow, and orange. With the fabric still wet, I applied a bit of Jacquard Metallic bronze paint. After an overnight of drying, the colors became lighter.

The head is needle sculpted from penne velvet. The ears are painted with metallic white paint and a small amount of blushing. To create the eyelids and mouth, I sculpted penne velvet and formed them with tacky glue. His whiskers are silk threads and wire that are curled around a bamboo skewer. I painted his driving gloves with bronze metallic paint and cut out holes for the knuckles; I used black metallic paint to create stitching lines.

The steering wheel is 15-gauge wire, wrapped with stiffened fabric and then painted. I made the carrot car out of muslin, dying the body orange, red, yellow, and green and the wheels black. I used a carrot stamp to create the spokes. His shoes also have wheels to help him around 'harepin' curves. Once my rabbit had gloves, I had my doll's theme. Now I just do my best to keep him under 65 m.p.h."

Fabrications

Working with Tyvek, liners, and machine embroidery

After coloring a blank canvas, it's time to move on and embellish it. This chapter explores how to use free-motion machine embroidery, Tyvek, bonding sheets, diaper liners, silk ribbon work, needle lace, the button hole stitch, knitting, and crochet to embellish your doll. Some of the fabrications you'll be familiar with, others you won't. The important thing to remember is that they all create beautiful effects and are great fun—you simply need to experiment with them to find which ones are your favorites.

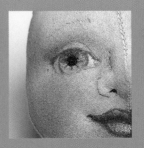

Intermediate Doll

Supplies for the Body

$^1/_3$ yard (30.5 cm) pima cotton

good-quality polyester thread

pins

scissors

stuffing

stuffing tools

pipe cleaners

long darning needle and strong thread

hemostats

hand-sewing needles

art supplies

two 25-mm wooden beads for legs

two 20-mm wooden beads for arms

paints and brushes

For this project, you'll use the second, intermediate doll pattern. This pattern has a bit more detail. The additional pattern pieces add more shape to the face and body. The doll becomes more like a puzzle, with you piecing the parts together to create a new look. This pattern introduces joints, which you can embellish. You'll create some articulated fingers. Even the foot starts to take on a more realistic shape.

Which fabric should you choose for her body? To give your doll a realistic look, you can make her from a flesh-colored fabric. Or you can dye the fabric after you've made the body, as explained in the previous chapter. To create a more fanciful look, you might consider using a batik fabric. Any type of fabric can be used to make a body— just make sure it has a tight weave and doesn't fray easily.

Arien, the sample doll (Doll #2), was created using a tightly woven pimatex cotton, which was then dyed. In this chapter, you'll discover many ways to embellish your doll's body and clothing. And because the face on this doll has greater dimension, you'll learn how to sculpt it to add even more detail.

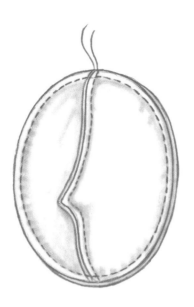

[step 3]
Sew all the way around.

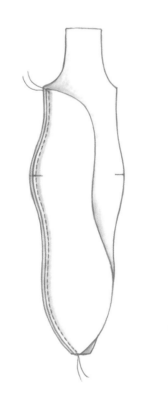

[step 5]
Sew from the center of the bust up
to the shoulder, then from the center of the
bust down to the bottom of the body.

Making the Body

1. Arrange and trace all patterns for Doll #2 onto the wrong side of the body fabric. (See Chapter 1, page 14.) Note those pattern pieces that have a seam allowance and those that don't.

2. Keep in mind that when doing the face and hands, you'll want to use a shorter stitch length on your sewing machine. Sew seam #1 on the Face and seam #2 on the Head Back, leaving open where marked. Cut out the two pieces. Open them up, and with right sides together, pin at the top of the head and at the chin.

3. Sew all the way around. Turn through the opening on the Head Back, and fill with enough stuffing so that the head is firm.

4. Sew seam #3 on the Body Back, leaving open where marked. Cut out all body pieces. (Keep in mind that if you use pinking shears, you won't have to clip curves.)

5. Matching the marks at the center of the bust, pin the Center Body Front to one Side Body Front piece. Sew from the center of the bust up to the shoulder, then from the center of the bust down to the bottom of the body.

   Do the same to the other Side Body Front piece. You now have a full body front.

6. Pin the Body Back to the full body front, and sew from the neck opening down the body and around up to the other side of the neck opening. Be sure to start out with a back stitch at the neck.

7. Turn the body right side out. Fill with enough stuffing so the body is firm. Be sure to plump up her breasts.

8. To stabilize the neck, place a pipe cleaner in it, but allow a bit of it to stick out so the head can rest on it. Close up the opening in the back with a ladder stitch, starting at the bottom of the opening and sewing up toward the top. When doing this, thread a long darning needle with about 1½ yards (1.5 m) of strong thread.

9. Attach the head to the neck by grabbing the neck with hemostats and pushing the neck into the opening at back of head. Ladder stitch the head to the neck.

10. Turning to the legs, sew from the opening at the knee all the way down to the opening at the toes on both sides of the Lower Leg. Cut out.

11. Fold the Lower Legs at the knees so the seams match. Sew along each tab, stopping short of the matched seams to leave an opening at the center.

12. For the feet, draw in a nice curve, as shown, and then sew, following your drawing.

13. Turn the Lower Leg through the opening at the top, and fill with stuffing. Close up the opening using a needle and thread.

14. The Upper Leg is sewn from the opening at the knee around the curve at the top and down to the other side of the opening.

15. Cut out the Upper Leg, fold at the knee, so the seams match. Sew along each tab, stopping short of the matched seam. Turn, and fill with stuffing. Close up the opening using a needle and thread.

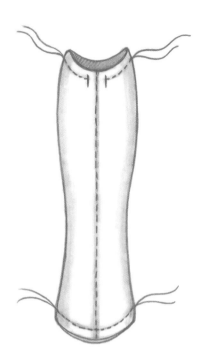

[step 11]
Sew tabs down to the center,
leaving them open at the center.

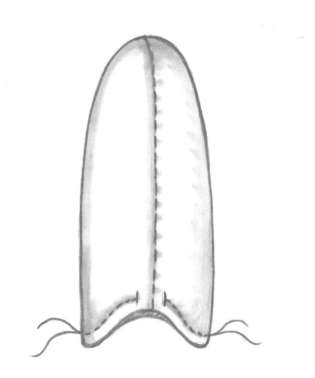

[step 15]
Close up the opening using
a needle and thread.

[step 16]
Join the Upper Leg to the
Lower Leg, using the beads.

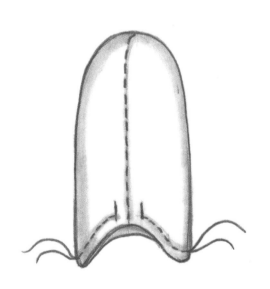

[step 19]
Fold the opening at the elbow
so the seams match. Sew across the tabs,
leaving it open at the center.

16. Paint the two 25-mm beads. After they're dry, join the Upper Leg to the Lower Leg, using the beads:

   a. Thread a needle with about $\frac{1}{2}$ yard (46 cm) of strong thread, and knot the end. Insert the needle at the end of one tab on the Upper Leg.

   b. Go through the bead and into the other side of the tab. Go through the tab and back through the bead to the other side. Do this three times.

   c. If you have enough thread, you can pick up the Lower Leg and do the same thing you did with the Upper Leg. You now have one full leg.

   d. Do the same with the other leg.

17. After your legs are done, attach them to the body, using about 1 yard (91.5 cm) of strong thread and a long needle. Follow the instructions in Chapter 2, page 25, on how to do this.

18. Turning to the arms, sew the Upper Arm from the opening at the elbow around to the other side of the opening. Then cut it out.

19. Fold the opening at the elbow so the seams match. Sew across the tabs, leaving it open at the center. Turn the arm right side out, and fill it with stuffing.

20. Sew the Lower Arm from the opening at the elbow all the way around the fingers and back up to the other side of the opening at the elbow. When sewing around the fingers, be sure to have two stitches across the tips and two stitches in between the fingers. (There are two fingers attached. Don't sew down the dashed lines yet.)

21. Cut out the Lower Arm, clipping in between the fingers and at the curves around the wrist. When clipping between the fingers, clip at each side and right up to the stitches, to help prevent wrinkling once the hands are turned.

22. Fold the arm at the elbow as you did with the Upper Arm, and sew across the tabs, leaving it open at the center.

23. To turn the fingers, use either your favorite turning tool or the tubes described in Chapter 1, page 15.

24. After you turn the fingers, topstitch down the center of the two fingers that are attached. Finish the hands as described in Chapter 2, page 24.

25. Attach the arms to the 20-mm beads as you did with the legs, and attach the arms to the body as you did with the legs.

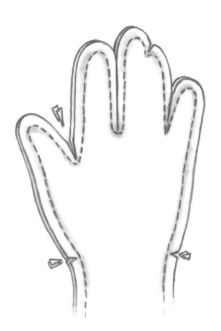

[step 20]
There are two fingers attached.
Don't sew down the dashed lines yet.

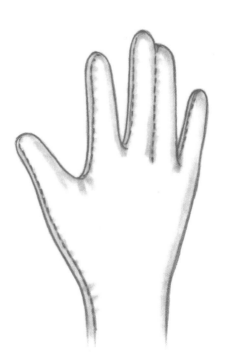

[step 24]
After you turn the fingers, topstitch down
the center of the two fingers that are attached.

Creating the Face

Follow the instructions in Chapter 1, pages 17 to 19, for grafting out and completing the face. (Because this doll has a center seam down her face, you don't have to worry about splitting it in half lengthwise.)

The photo below illustrates how the doll's face should be grafted. The left side shows more of the grafting and the right side the finished look. Once you outline your features with a brown fabric pen, you can erase all pencil marks.

Sculpting

Before coloring the doll's face, you'll want to sculpt it, using a needle and thread. As you go from one area to another, pull on your thread. However, look at the doll's face as you pull, because you don't want to pull so tight that you cause wrinkling—you simply want to define the features. Follow the steps below to work your way around the face:

1. Thread a long darning needle with 1 yard (91.5 m) of strong thread. The thread should be in a single strand, not doubled. Anchor this at the back of the doll's head.

2. Push the needle through the head and out the inside corner of an eye (**#1**).

3. Push the needle back inside the head at the corner of the eye and come out at the opposite nostril (**#2**).

4. Push the needle back inside the head at the nostril and come out at the opposite flare of the nose (**#3**).

5. Push the needle back inside at the flare and come out straight across at the opposite flare (**#4**).

6. Push the needle back inside at the flare and come out at the opposite nostril (**#5**).

7. Push the needle back inside at the nostril and come out at the opposite inside corner of the eye (**#6**).

8. Push the needle back inside at the corner of the eye and come out at the outside corner of the mouth (**#7**).

9. Push the needle back inside at the outside corner of the mouth and come out at the outside corner of the eye (**#8**).

10. Push the needle back inside at the outside corner of the eye and come out at the inside corner of the other eye (**#1**).

11. Push the needle back inside at the inside corner of the eye and come out at the outside corner of the mouth (**#9**).

12. Push the needle back inside at the outside corner of the mouth and come out at the outside corner of the eye (**#10**).

13. Push the needle back inside at the corner of the eye and come out at the back of the head, then anchor off.

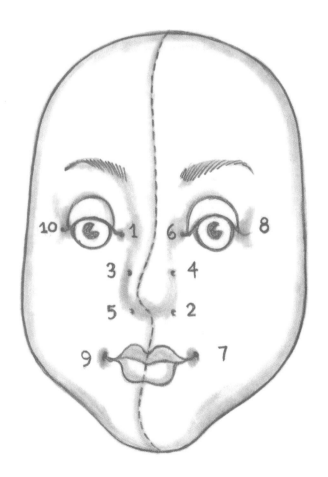

Numbers on the above face correspond to the bold numbers in the text on the left.

Adding Color

To color the face, follow the steps laid out in Chapter 2, page 26. Add shadows and highlights using the colored pencils.

Then color the eyes and lips with the colored pencils. Outline everything with the fabric pens, and add your highlights to the eyes with the white gel roller. The side-by-side comparison in the photos on the left show you the before and after.

Color in the irises with the lightest shade, then use the medium shade under the eyelid and down the side that is in the shadow. Use the darkest shade for under the upper eyelid.

After you finish the doll's face, set it with heat, using an iron.

Supplies for the Embellishments

$^1/_4$ *yard (23 cm) velvet for skirt*

wood block or rubber stamp

iron

diaper liner (Gerber EZ-liner) or disposable diaper

crayons

baking parchment

rayon and metallic sewing threads

$^3/_8$" *(0.9 cm) silk ribbon*

doilies

needle and thread

$^1/_4$ *yard (23 cm) silk chiffon*

dye

double-sided bonding sheet

glitzy yarns and threads

hot air gun

strong water-soluble stabilizer

fabric-weight and medium-weight Tyvek

acrylic or fabric paint or markers

wooden barbecue skewers

$^1/_4$" *(0.6 cm) washers*

tapestry needle

size 4 knitting needles

size D crochet hook

aluminum foil

darning or free-motion foot

beading wire

Embellishing the Doll

Clothing and embellishing the doll is the fun part. There are so many new techniques and ideas available. In this section we'll explore several. The dolls in the Gallery section that follows include all of the techniques discussed in this chapter, making them a great source of inspiration.

Transferring Colors and Images

Along with a few basic supplies, a diaper liner can help you transfer color and images onto your doll's skirt in no time at all. If you can't find a box of diaper liners and you don't have a box of disposable diapers handy, ask a friend, relative, or neighbor who does. All it takes is one diaper liner. (Disposable diapers have a lining inside that's the same as the EZ-liners.)

The skirt needs to be done first because it's attached first. Cut a 20" x 8" (51 x 20.5 cm) piece from the ¼ yard (23 cm) of velvet. Lay it down on an ironing board, velvet side up.

If you have a wood block, that will work best. (If you don't, use a large rubber stamp.) Lay the diaper liner on top of the wood block. Pick out the color of crayon you want, and rub it on the diaper liner. You'll see the design transfer to the liner. Then lay the diaper liner on top of the velvet, crayon side up. Lay a piece of baking parchment on top, and iron over the design area with the iron on the highest setting. Hold the iron in place for about 10 seconds, then move to the next area. Lift up the baking parchment to ensure that the image transfers. Some irons aren't as hot as others, so you may have to go over the image again.

The diaper liner melts into the velvet, leaving the design from your rubbing. Although this technique can be used on other fabrics, it works best on velvet. Also, some people recommend grease markers (Shiva Markers), but crayons seem to work far better. Plus they're easy to find, and they're inexpensive. You'll go through a crayon very quickly, depending on how large a design you want.

Using Free-Motion Machine Embroidery

Sewing-machine embroidery can add your unique mark of creativity to almost anything you make. It is fun, easy, and faster than hand embroidery. Almost any thread will work if the sewing machine is properly adjusted. Experiment to find threads that work best with your machine. Correct thread tension is very important. Usually, the top tension needs to be looser than the bottom. Adjust the machine to allow the bottom tension to pull the top thread down even with the underside of the material. It should not be loose enough to cause loops on the wrong side of your work.

To prepare the machine, remove the presser foot, put on a darning or free motion foot, and lower the feed dog. (On some machines, a lever may raise the throat plate to keep the feed dog from interfering with stitching.) Then, set the machine stitch length and width controls on "O". Always test the stitch tension and setting before beginning your project.

To begin stitching, use the hand-wheel, insert the needle into the fabric, and bring up the bobbin thread. Holding threads taut, take three or four small stitches to lock the threads in place. Clip off the loose thread ends. Continue stitching following any of these basic movements: moving vertically or horizontally, back and forth across the fabric, or moving in small circular or swirl patterns. The movements can form distinct rows of stitches, as shown in the skirt design that follows, or they may be blended by overlapping. To end stitching, move the stitch width regulator to "O". Then, stitch three or four stitches in the same place. Pull the threads to the wrong side, and clip close to the fabric. You can also combine or overlap straight stitches and zigzag stitches.

Adding Ribbons, Silk Strips, and Lace

Once you add a splash of color to your doll's skirt, you can embellish it even more using a few basic techniques. The sample doll skirt here used free-motion machine embroidery, silk ribbons, lace motifs (from an old doily), and torn silk strips to add interest.

Start by placing some variegated rayon thread in your machine and any thread in the bobbin. (The thread in the bobbin won't show.) Starting at the top of the fabric, stitch up and down the length of the skirt. When you're ready to add a silk ribbon or torn silk strip, start at the top and gather the ribbon or strip as illustrated. Continue down the length of the skirt. You can add some strips at the bottom of the skirt and bunch them up tighter.

To add a lace motif, position a doily on the skirt wherever you want that design, and then topstitch it in place.

Finishing the Skirt

Once you have your skirt the way you want it, sew up the back seam and sew in a hem. (If you like, you can use decorative stitching for this.) Then sew a running stitch along the waist. Slip the skirt on the body and pull the threads at the waist to fit. Secure the threads by tying in an overhand knot then tack skirt to waist using a needle and thread.

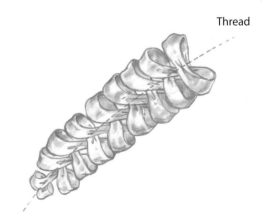

Thread

When you're ready to add a silk ribbon or torn silk strip, start at the top and gather the ribbon or strip.

53

Adding Glitz to the Bodice

Although the following technique happened by accident, it added glitz to the bodice just beautifully. To begin, tear two 10" x 4" (25.5 x 10 cm) pieces of silk chiffon. Dye them to match the doll's color scheme. As they dry (they'll do so fairly quickly), cut two pieces of double-sided bonding sheet the same size. Peel off the backing on one side of one sheet, and lay the sheet down on an ironing board, sticky side up. Throw bits and pieces of glitzy yarns and threads onto the sheet. Peel off the backing on one side of the second sheet, and lay this on top of your glitzy layer. With your iron on the highest setting, iron the two sheets together, creating a sandwich of glitz.

Set the sandwich aside, and lay down a piece of baking parchment on the ironing board. Place one chiffon piece onto the parchment. Peel off the backing from both sides of the sandwich, and place it down on the chiffon. Put the other piece of chiffon on top of the sandwich. Then put a piece of baking parchment on top of that. With the iron set at the highest setting, press one section at a time until your sandwich is ironed to itself.

Topstitch the silk chiffon sandwich with variegated rayon thread in a random fashion. Then carefully burn it with a hot air gun. You don't want to set it on fire: You simply want to char the silk, to expose the glitzy threads underneath and create a velvety effect.

Finish the bodice by using free-motion machine embroidery edging along the bottom. Place a piece of water-soluble stabilizer under the silk, then stitch. You'll want to start off with some straight stitches and then lock in your design by crossing over each one several times with some short zigzag stitches.

Place the bodice in room temperature water, and dissolve the stabilizer. Let the bodice air dry. Set it aside for now.

Creating Tyvek Beads

Tyvek is part paper and part fiber, so it doesn't tear easily. Express Mail and FedEx envelopes are made from medium-weight Tyvek; clothing and environmental suits, from fabric-weight Tyvek; and housing insulation, from heavy-weight Tyvek. For doll making, medium-weight and fabric-weight Tyvek are best. You'll want to avoid using the heavy-weight Tyvek because it has chemicals in it. (See Resources, page 118.)

Cut some strips of Tyvek, and color both sides with acrylic or fabric paints, crayons, or markers. Let dry.

Cut these in smaller pieces of varying shapes, about 1" x 3" (2.5 x 7.5 cm). Wrap about three of the shapes and colors onto a wooden skewer, securing them with metallic thread. Using the lower setting on a hot air gun, melt the Tyvek together, to create a beautiful bead.

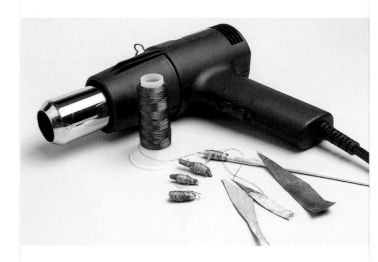

Using the lower setting on a
hot air gun, melt the Tyvek together,
to create a beautiful bead.

Carefully remove the bead from the skewer and make as many as you need to embellish the doll.

Take some Tyvek beads, and string them on some yarn. Tie several overhand knots in the ends to keep the beads from falling off the yarn. Topstitch these to the bottom of the bodice.

Applying Covered Washers

Hardware stores are a great place to find unique doll-making supplies. Washers are a good example. Eileen Lyons was the source on this one; see her doll in the Gallery, page 60.

First you'll need to cover the washers, using some yarn that matches the doll's outfit and a tapestry needle. The stitch used to cover the washers is called "button hole." If you don't know it, it's extremely easy to learn.

Leave the yarn on the spool. Thread the cut end through the tapestry needle, leaving about 1 yard (91.5 cm) to work with. (This means you'll pull 1 yard (91.5 cm) of the yarn off the spool.) Take the needle through the inside of the washer, and come up and under the loose end. Go back through the center of the washer and up under the loose end. Continue doing this until you've gone completely around the washer. Cut the yarn from the spool, and tie at the washer and again at the top. Topstitch this onto the bodice. Make as many covered washers as you want, and attach them to the bodice or leave some for other parts of the clothing.

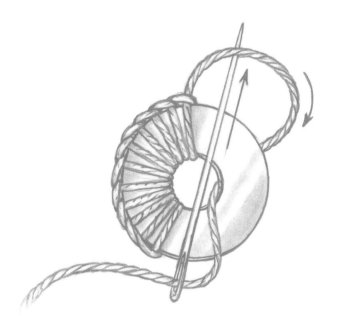

Cover the washers using the "button hole stitch."

Completing the Bodice

Once the bodice is embellished to your liking, pin it to the doll's body. Overlap the raw ends at her back, and ladder stitch or whipstitch it closed. Tuck in here and there using a needle and thread. Because the bodice is so embellished, the threads won't show.

Making Sleeves

The sample doll's sleeves were knitted and then finished with a crocheted edging. An alternative is to create sleeves from fabric. To recreate the knitted look, follow the steps below:

1. Using size 4 knitting needles, cast on 33.

2. Knit 29 rows.

3. Row 30: Knit 3, knit 2 together, repeat 5 times, knit 3.

4. Row 31: Knit.

5. Row 32: Knit 3, knit 2 together, repeat 4 times, knit 2.

6. Row 33: Knit.

7. Bind off, and leave a 7" (18 cm) tail.

8. Thread the yarn through a tapestry needle, and sew the sides together to form the sleeve.

9. To create the edging, anchor glitzy yarn at the bottom of the sleeve with a size D crochet hook. Chain 3. In the starting stitch of the knitted edge, double crochet 2 times. In the next stitch of the sleeve edge, double crochet 3 times. Continue around the edge of the sleeve with 3 double crochets in each stitch, to create a lacy effect.

10. Slip the sleeves onto the doll, and tack them to the shoulders using a needle and thread.

Creating Tyvek Clusters

Paint some light-weight or fabric-weight Tyvek using the colors of your choice. Let dry. Cut out various shapes. Hold these down on tile or aluminum foil with a wooden skewer, and apply heat with a hot air gun. The shapes will curl up on themselves. As you heat them, you can move them around with the skewer. Set them aside to cool.

Apply the clusters to the doll's sleeves to add interest. You might also place some on her head and add some Tyvek beads to the clusters as a further embellishment. The Tyvek remains soft, so you can sew the clusters using a regular needle and thread.

Creating Shoes

Trace the shoe pattern onto a piece of water-soluble stabilizer. Trace two for each foot for a total of four. Then trace two soles.

Place metallic thread in your bobbin and variegated rayon thread in your machine. Lower your feed dog, and use a darning foot or free-motion foot in your machine. (Keep in mind that when doing free-motion machine embroidery, you don't want the foot to touch the plate of the machine.)

Sew the outline of the shoes, then sew in a grid. The grid lays down a base that will prevent your decorative or free motion stitches from falling apart after the stabilizer is removed. To create a grid, stitch horizontally, back and forth across the piece from one side of the outline to the other. Then, stitch vertically, up and down the piece, to create perpendicular lines across the rows, thereby creating a grid. Dissolve the stabilizer.

When the pieces are dry, hand sew the top of the shoes together, and place them on the doll's feet. Hand sew the soles to the bottoms of the shoes while they're on her feet. Catch her feet occasionally to secure them.

Giving the Doll Wings

Trace two wings onto the water-soluble stabilizer. Sew along the outline, then do the grid work. After the grid work is done, set your machine to the zigzag stitch, and fill in the centers of the design.

When the wings are to your liking, zigzag over some beading wire to stabilize them. Then put them in water to dissolve away the stabilizer. When the wings are dry, tack them to the doll's back.

Adding Cuffs to the Wrists

Draw a design on the stabilizer and free-motion machine embroider. When you're done, put the cuffs in water to dissolve away the stabilizer. When they're dry, tack them onto the doll's arms.

Attaching Hair to the Head

On the sample doll, mohair was used. Cluster the mohair, and sew it along the hairline. Fluff it up and arrange it using a felting needle or a needle and thread. Sew some Tyvek clusters toward the front of her hairline. Then add some Tyvek beads.

What a beauty!

Take Me to the Tropics

ARTIST: Barbara Carleton Evans   (Pattern: Doll #1)

"Take me to the Tropics (I've had enough of Winter) began in my fabric stash. I wanted something attention-grabbing, so I chose purple suede and used it to sew the doll on the machine. To transfer the pattern to suede, I cut pattern pieces out of freezer paper, ironed them onto the wrong side of the suede, placed that suede piece on top of another suede piece (right sides together), and machine stitched around the pattern. After stitching, I trimmed each piece and peeled off the freezer paper pattern. (Thanks to Louise Mendenhall for that nifty trick.) Because of the stiffness of the suede, I didn't thread-wrap the elbow joints. I attached the arms just like the legs. Before assembling the body, I lightly brushed the surfaces with stenciling paint.

I used natural fiber yarns for hair, hand-dyed by Kate Stephenson. The hair ornaments began with a little green parrot. After attaching him, I added bits and pieces. The tube bead is made from a rolled up postage stamp (first class, of course).

The doll's garment is a loosely crocheted neck scarf. The purple metallic yarn looks good with the doll's body color. The combination of the body color, garment color, and the parrot gave the doll a neat tropical theme.

Finally, I added postage stamps, costume jewelry pins, green glass leaf-shaped beads, vintage fabric flowers, and buttons to embellish the body, and I cut the guitar player from the back of an old playing card."

Arianne

ARTIST: Di McDonald   (Pattern: Doll #1)

"What fun this doll was to make! At first I planned to straighten her legs and wire her body so she could stand and show off her clothes. After thinking about it a little I decided to go with the pattern and change the joints and hands. I especially loved her feet: She looked so graceful, just like a ballerina. Bright colors are my favorites, so I chose a very fine bright orange silk, which was shot with hot pink. To go with this I found some hot pink chiffon, Tyvek, assorted threads, yarns, beads, and sequins.

Wrapping is one of the techniques I am playing with right now, so after I made the body, I ripped strips of silk and wrapped the arms, legs, and body. I left her belly button showing to give her a trendier look. Over this I used metallic threads. I also painted a sheet of Tyvek with Lumiere paints, ripped more strips of the silk, and glued them to the Tyvek. I then cut the Tyvek into strips and rolled them into beads. I used embossing powder and a heat gun to give the beads unusual shapes. These beads made great edging for the off-center neckline and the skirt. The rest of the beads I threaded onto copper wire and made a belt.

I painted the ballet slippers with Lumiere paints, and I used various sequins and beads to decorate them. I added multiple gathered skirts using the silk, chiffon, and white tulle. I scrunched, sequined, and beaded the sleeves, and gathered and flounced the silk at her wrists.

Black maribu seemed appropriate for her hair, and to top it off I made a turban for her head. Lots of bright colors brought this doll's pretty face to life!"

Gussie of Somerset

ARTIST: Eileen Lyons (Pattern: Doll #2)

"Using a new dye/fabric paint I colored Tyvek, interfacing, seam binding, cheesecloth, crochet thread, fabric. When everything was colored, I started to play. I used the cheese-cloth and the Tyvek to create her blouse. Then I cut the inter-facing and some fabric into triangle shapes, threw them onto a piece of fabric, and started to free-motion machine embroider them. The doll now had her skirt.

For one sleeve, I dyed a piece of lightweight fabric. Then I pulled out the crochet hook and some funky yarns and started to do some free-form crocheting. She ended up with a funky sleeve and hat. For her hair I used some eyelash yarn. Then I crocheted her shoes.

To embellish her, I stitched the plastic rings that you use as markers when you knit from her hat. Finally, I added beaded flowers and leaves on her shoes and some beads and threads around her neckline.

Because I used a lot of yarn and thread, I wanted to name the doll after my aunt in England who was a wonderful yarn artist. Her full name is Augusta of Midsummer-Norton, Somerset NR Bath. I shortened it to Gussie of Somerset."

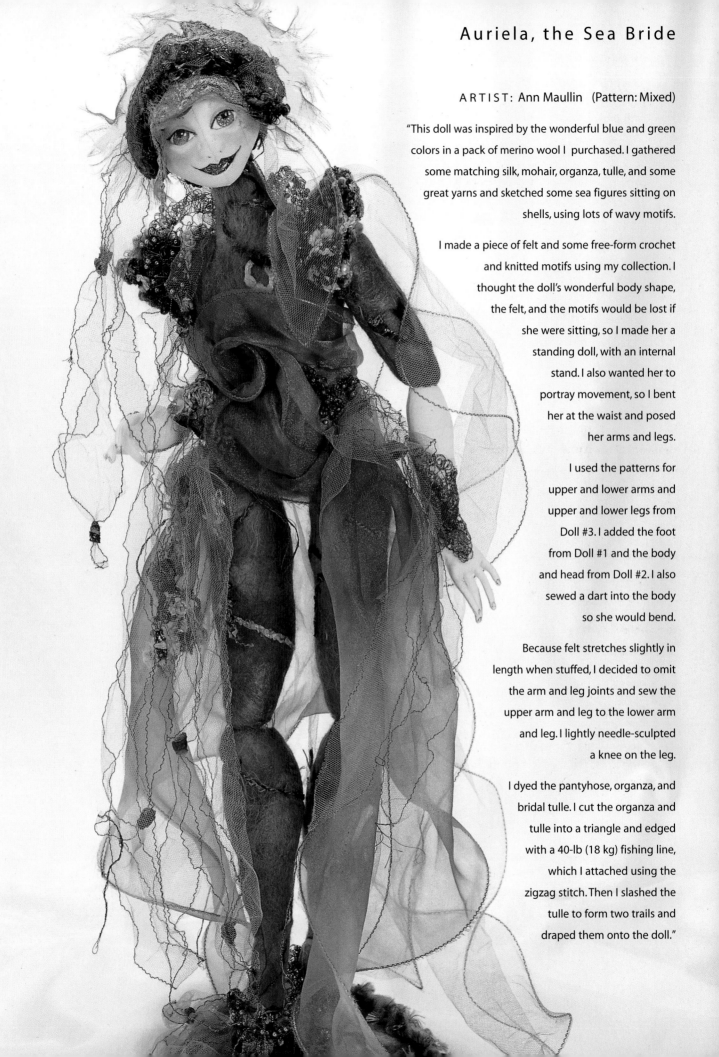

Auriela, the Sea Bride

ARTIST: Ann Maullin   (Pattern: Mixed)

"This doll was inspired by the wonderful blue and green colors in a pack of merino wool I purchased. I gathered some matching silk, mohair, organza, tulle, and some great yarns and sketched some sea figures sitting on shells, using lots of wavy motifs.

I made a piece of felt and some free-form crochet and knitted motifs using my collection. I thought the doll's wonderful body shape, the felt, and the motifs would be lost if she were sitting, so I made her a standing doll, with an internal stand. I also wanted her to portray movement, so I bent her at the waist and posed her arms and legs.

I used the patterns for upper and lower arms and upper and lower legs from Doll #3. I added the foot from Doll #1 and the body and head from Doll #2. I also sewed a dart into the body so she would bend.

Because felt stretches slightly in length when stuffed, I decided to omit the arm and leg joints and sew the upper arm and leg to the lower arm and leg. I lightly needle-sculpted a knee on the leg.

I dyed the pantyhose, organza, and bridal tulle. I cut the organza and tulle into a triangle and edged with a 40-lb (18 kg) fishing line, which I attached using the zigzag stitch. Then I slashed the tulle to form two trails and draped them onto the doll."

Tarni, Barrier Reef Princess

ARTIST: Wendy Fenwick (Pattern: Doll #3)

"For me, Tarni depicts the glorious colors of Australia and the textures of the Great Barrier Reef. Her 'royal robe' uses many techniques, textures, and colors to capture the beautiful coral beds and reef life. Her dress is made from crinkled silky fabric, to look like water glistening in the sun and pooling around her feet.

I used various fabrics, yarns, laces, silk ribbons, and embroideries, dying them when necessary to match my color palette. I chose the clear blue silk fabric for the robe, overlaying darker blue lace around the bottom edge for depth. I appliquéd tulle for seaweed. I added knitting and crochet yarns for coral shapes and robe 'fur' edging trim for textural effect.

Before I arranged my design and colors, I made many wide ruffles to give the seaweed a 3-D effect. These strips consisted of dyed silks, metallics, and organzas, cut on the bias, doubled in half, with fishing line inside the fold and fancy threads satin stitched along the fold edge of ruffle. I sewed the raw edges with a gathering stitch pulled tight to flute the fabrics. I tucked in knitted and crocheted fancy yarns for coral.

I appliquéd all embroidered designs with transparent thread and completed Tarni's ensemble with little sandals, made from felted merino fleece and silk fibers, dyed to match water colors, and beaded.

Finally, I adorned her starfish crown and necklace with crystals and seed beads and her sea horse with topaz chips and crystal eyes."

Huldra, Troll Maiden

ARTIST: Ute Vasina   (Pattern: Doll #3)

"Considering that I'm used to making all my dolls from doe suede and with troll-like features, this doll posed an interesting challenge. The first thing I did was make her nose larger. (I have this thing about noses.) The next step was the torso. I really liked the womanly figure! She didn't resemble any of my troll figures. I decided she would be 'Huldra,' appearing like a fair maiden—a beautiful seductress from the outside, but very much a troll from within. After all, some female trolls will do that to find or catch a husband.

With this is mind, she took on a great form, right down to her toes. I almost hated putting clothes on her. With her strong personality, I had a sense right from the start what she wanted, so her clothes are very simple, her sweater hand-knit, and her hair made from mohair.

Finally, I love to recycle old or used things. For some dolls, I'll use a piece of clothing. For others, I'll add something old, such as an old skeleton key, a piece of jewelry, or another great find. In Huldra's hand I've placed a very special key.

This doll has a real peaceful elegance about her. Maybe it's the beauty shining from within."

Beading

Doing peyote beadwork and bead embroidery

4

Beading can add a wonderful level of embellishment to your doll creations. In addition to using Tyvek beads, which were featured in the last chapter, you'll learn to make wrapped beads and peyote flowers and do other types of free-form beading. Beads can be used for everything from simple, delicate adornments to more elaborate ones like the obsessive beauty of a beaded mermaid's tail, as seen on page 79.

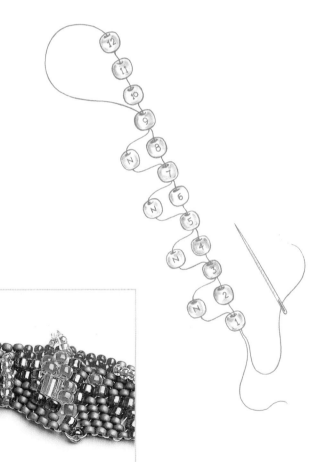

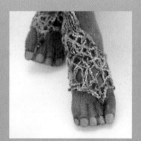

"I love the story of my name! Now, tell me about *Alma*, Daddy. Where does that come from?"

"I picked the name *Alma* just for you. You are the first and the only Alma. You will make your own story."

ALMA
Sofia
ESPERANZA
JOSÉ
Pura
Candela!

"That's my name, and it fits me just right!
I am Alma, and I have a story to tell."

A Note from Juana

My name is Juana Carlota Martinez Pizarro. My father named me *Juana* after his mother, Juana Francisca. My mother chose the name *Carla* to honor the memory of her uncle, Carlos. My father was a man of decisions, so when it was time to register my birth, he changed *Carla* to *Carlota* on the birth certificate. He was convinced that *Juana Carlota* was the mighty name he wanted for his daughter. Thanks to that change, I got stuck with what I thought was the most old-fashioned, harsh, ugly, and way-too-Spanish name in all of Lima, Peru, where I grew up! Little did I know that later on, after I moved to the United States, it would feel unique and remind me every day of where I come from.

What is the story of your name?
What story would you like to tell?

To Victor Nicolás Martínez Gómez, my dad

First edition 2018

Library of Congress Catalog Card Number 2018935034
ISBN 978-0-7636-9355-8 (English hardcover)
ISBN 978-0-7636-9358-9 (Spanish hardcover)

19 20 21 22 23 CGB 10 9 8 7

Printed in Mankato, MN, U.S.A.

This book was typeset in Youbee.
The illustrations were done with graphite, colored pencils,
and print transfers on handmade textured paper.

Candlewick Press
99 Dover Street
Somerville, Massachusetts 02144

visit us at www.candlewick.com